The Sunny day Book

Jane Bull

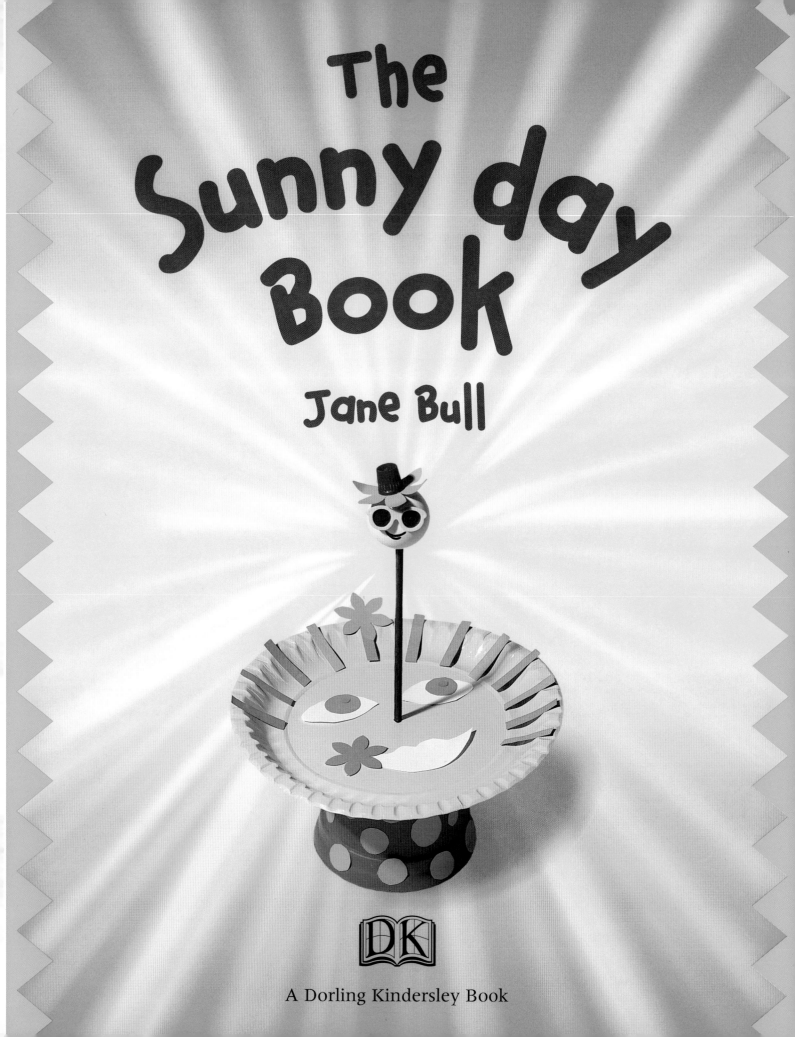

DK

A Dorling Kindersley Book

LONDON, NEW YORK, MUNICH,
MELBOURNE, AND DELHI

DESIGN • Jane Bull
EDITOR • Penelope Arlon
PHOTOGRAPHY • Andy Crawford
DESIGN ASSISTANCE • Sadie Thomas

PUBLISHING MANAGER • Sue Leonard
MANAGING ART EDITOR • Clare Shedden
PRODUCTION • Shivani Pandey
DTP DESIGNER • Almudena Díaz

For Charlotte, Billy, and James

First published in Great Britain in 2004 by
Dorling Kindersley Limited
80 Strand, London WC2R 0RL

A Penguin Company

2 4 6 8 10 9 7 5 3

A CIP catalogue record for this book
is available from the British Library

ISBN: 1-4053-0243-7

Colour reproduction by
GRB Editrice S.r.l., Verona, Italy
Printed and bound in China by Toppan

See our complete
catalogue at
www.dk.com

Keep your cool
in the sunshine

In this Sunny book you'll find...

hundreds of reasons...

to get outdoors!

Sunny time

Track the sun as it moves across the sky, and keep track of time.

Is it time for a drink?

8
9
10
11
midday 12
1
2
3
4
5
6
7

Sundials

As the sun moves across the sky, believe it or not it can tell you the time. Stand something tall, such as a stick, in a bucket of sand in an area that gets sunlight all day. Each hour place a shell where the shadow of the stick falls and note down what time it is. The next day you can tell the time by using it!

Fun times in the sun

All you need is a bright sunny day and some things to mark the hours as they pass. If you are on a beach use shells – and turn over to learn how to make a sundial for your garden.

midday
12
11   1
10   2
9   3
8   4
          5
          6
7

Make a clock wherever you are.

Check your clock time after time

Making time

Try putting the shells on the tip of the stick shadow and at the end of the day see what shape you have made. It might not quite be circular like a watch. That's weird! If you make the sundial out of pebbles or shells then you can leave it out all year round. Does it work at all times of the year?

5

Sun clock

Time to watch the clock in the garden.

what's the time?

Impress your friends by being able to tell the time without looking at a watch. How do you do it? By using the sun.

How to make a clock

You will need:

- Paper plate
- Terracotta plant pot
- Stick or garden cane
- A watch
- Strips of paper
- Sticky tack

Before you assemble your sun clock, decorate the plate, stick, and pot.

Put sticky tack around the hole.

Press the plate onto the sticky tack.

1. Make a hole in the centre of the plate and push the cane through.

2. Now put the cane through the hole in the plant pot.

3. Make sure the plate doesn't turn easily on the stick.

use the sunlight to set your clock

You will need a whole sunny day to set your clock so that you can read it the next day.

1. Place your clock in a sunny area.

2. The stick will cast a shadow across the plate. This is the sun telling you the time.

10 o'clock   12 o'clock   2 o'clock

Midday 12

It's just past 3 o'clock

3. Now look at your watch, and mark the shadow on each hour with a strip of paper. For example at 10 o'clock mark the shadow, then continue until the sun goes down.

4. The next day, tell the time by seeing where the shadow falls!

Make the 12 o'clock strip look different to remind you where it is.

7

Take cover

Stay out of the sun in a home-made hide-away.

Keep the enemy away!

No entry unless you know the password

keep out

Beware!

When the sun is getting too hot and you need some shade, don't go indoors – build a tent in the garden with some blankets and garden canes.

Picnic pots

Setting up camp

Once you've made your camp, you will need food supplies. Hang clear notices, such as flags or a sign, to make sure that visitors are unwelcome unless invited. Create a password for your friends.

9

Setting up camp

The whole idea of a camp is to put it somewhere where you won't be disturbed, and bring plenty of rations with you to keep you going. The beauty of this tent is that you can fold it up, store it, and use it again and again.

For the camp you will need

- 12 bamboo canes
- Strong tape and scissors
- An old blanket or rug
- Clothes pegs

Tape the sticks together

Lay out the bamboo canes in the position shown and tape each corner and the centre securely.

1.5 m (5 ft)

1.2 m (4 ft)

1.8 m (6 ft)

1.2 m (4 ft)

1.8 m (6 ft)

You will need two of these frames for the hideout.

1.5 m (5 ft)

Wrap the tape round and round to make sure the frame is secure.

Complete your hideaway

You will need a friend to help you hold them up.

Make 2 of these

Stand the two frames up in a triangle shape and tape the two top ends together tightly.

Make sure you make the hideout wide enough to fit inside.

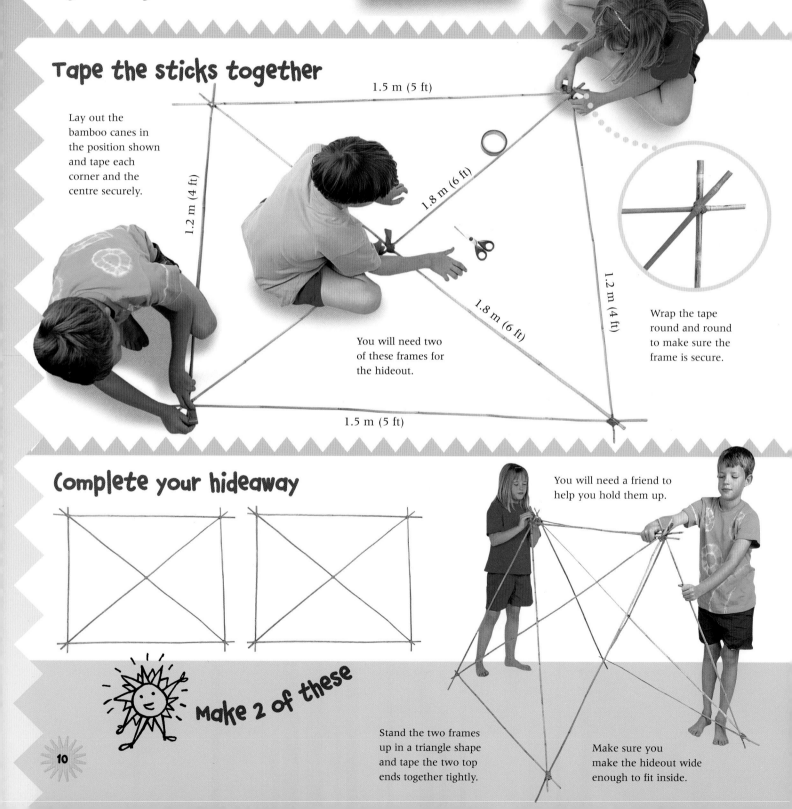

BAMBOO CANES

4 canes at
1.2 m (4 ft)

4 canes at
1.5 m (5 ft)

4 canes at
1.8 m
(6 ft)

Bamboo canes

You will need 12 bamboo canes to make your hideout. If you need to cut them, ask an adult to help you.

Fly the flag

• 1 bamboo cane
• A piece of scrap material
• String

Paint a design on your flag and snip down the edges to make a zig-zag pattern. Then bunch up two corners and tie them to the pole with string.

Picnic bowl

• 3 x 60 cm (2 ft) bamboo canes
• Strong tape, plastic bowl

Tie the three poles together in the centre, let them go, and pop a plastic bowl on top. Fill with rations.

Tie the poles tightly in the middle.

When you let go of the poles they should fall into a stool shape and balance perfectly on three legs.

Drape the rug or blanket over the top of the framework.

Password please!

Make a "no entry" sign out of cardboard for privacy.

Use clothes pegs to attach the rug to the frame at the bottom.

Picnic in a pot

Look, no left-overs!

Edible pots

Anything delicious can be put into an ice cream cone – sweet or savoury snacks. Perfect for picnics, no mess to clear up!

popcorn

Surprise pots

Spoon delicious dips into
the bottom of your pots
and put fruit or
vegetables on top.

Cream cheese dip

yogurt or cream

Taramasalata

Mayonnaise

13

Cover up!

Wear your art on your clothes, and keep the sun off too!

GraffiT-shirt

Make your mark

Fabric pens are the easiest way to decorate a T-shirt. Draw your design straight on, then iron it to make it permanent.

Remember to put paper or card inside the T-shirt to stop the ink going through.

You will need:
• White or light-coloured cotton T-shirt
• Fabric pens

I'm looking at you!

T-shirts

White and pale-coloured T-shirts work best when decorating or dying. If you use a dark T-shirt the decoration won't show as clearly. So get out your old T-shirts and cover up!

Hey! Look at me I look good like that.

Pack up all your stuff in me!

Transform your clothes

Crazy faces

You could use any material to decorate your hats and bags, but felt is a great one to use. It is easy to cut and can be stuck onto other material easily using PVA or fabric glue.

Practise your face shapes on newspaper first. Then cut them out.

Use the paper templates to draw on to the fabric.

Cut out the shapes.

what to do
• Practise your shapes on a piece of newspaper.
• Use your newspaper template to cut out the felt shapes.
• Glue them into position.

Glue the shapes.

PVA glue

Stick into position.

You will need:
• Scraps of fabric, such as felt
• Newspaper
• Scissors
• PVA or fabric glue

16

Tie-dye T-shirts

The secret of tie-dye is the elastic bands. By tying them tightly the dye will not colour the tied bits, leaving swirls of pattern. When you are dying fabrics, make sure you read and follow the instructions on the dye packet.

⭐ **Ask an adult** to help with hot water.

Tie the bands

Scrunch up pieces of your T-shirt and tie elastic bands tightly to each little scrunch.

Follow the guidelines on the packet.

Now dunk your T-shirt into the dye and leave for however long the instructions tell you. Use rubber gloves.

Take it out and rinse it

Mix up the dye

Dunk in a T-shirt

Remove the bands

Rinse the T-shirt until the colour stops running out. Remove the elastic bands to reveal the twisty, swirly pattern. Then hang it up in the sun to dry.

Remember to use a light T-shirt otherwise the dye won't show.

The more elastic bands you use, the more patterns you get.

Thirst aid

Instant lemon soothies

to be taken in emergencies.

Lemon remedy contains:

3 MEDIUM LEMONS   +   I LITRE WATER   +   SUGAR   =

Now sit back and take it squeezy!

Fizzy lemonade

For extra fizz, dilute your lemonade with fizzy mineral water.

Lemon popsicles

Lemon twister

A sugary candy twist with a slice of lemon in the middle makes a perfect stirrer.

Ice cube lemonpops

crusty, sugary rim

Long cool lemon

Fill a tall glass with lots of ice and let it melt away into your lemonade.

ways to add sweetness

• Use candy canes and lollypops as stirrers.

• For a yummy, sugary crust on the rim of the glass, tip out some sugar on to a plate. Hold a glass upside down and dip the rim into water then into the sugar. Leave it to dry.

Lemon take-away

Re-use empty drinks bottles and fill them up with a batch of home-made lemonade.

19

Thirst aid kit

This lemonade recipe will make just over one litre. It may be tangy so add sugar or extra water until it tastes good. The best thing to do is experiment.

Remember to save some to make ice lollies and ice cubes.

Drink up

Your lemonade will only keep for two days in the fridge. So make sure you drink it quickly!

Squeeze to meet you

THE THIRST AID KIT

CHOPPING BOARD

FUNNEL

LARGE SPOON

SHARP KNIFE

BLENDER

LARGE JUG OR BOWL

MEASURING JUG

SIEVE

Making lemonade

Scrub all the lemons well as you will be using the whole fruit – even the peel!

- 3 lemons
- 1 litre water
- Sugar to taste

☆ **Ask an adult** to help with the blender.

1 Wash the lemons and chop each into eight pieces.

2 Put the lemons into a blender and add some of the water.

3 Blend until the mixture is smooth.

Ice cube lollies

Place some fruit lollies into an ice cube tray and simply top up with your lemonade. Put them into the freezer over night and you have ice-cold, fruity lemonade lollipops!

 4 Pour the mixture into a sieve.

5 Let the juice drain through, by pressing it with the back of a spoon.

Sugar ... _and water_

6 Add some sugar to taste and the remaining water.

It's best to keep your lemonade in a bottle in the fridge.

Gently pour through a funnel.

Hold on tight to the bottle.

 7 Bottle your lemonade.

Bowls of ice

Bowls of ice that keep things chilled in the hot sun

Ice bowl tips

• To remove your ice bowl, leave it out at room temperature for a while to loosen it.

• Put the ice bowl back into the freezer for a few minutes to cool it again.

• Remember the bowl will melt in the hot sun so eat up!

Freeze an ice bowl

Keep your food and drinks cool in a chilly ice bowl. You could use other fruit around the edges or even flowers and leaves.

1. Place a smaller bowl inside a larger one. Cut two lemons into thin slices and position them in the gap between the bowls.

2. Fill the gap with water. Place a stone in the centre of the small bowl and tape it securely to the larger bowl to hold it in place.

3. Put it into the freezer overnight. When you take it out, leave it out and let it melt slightly. Gently remove the bowls to reveal your ice bowl!

Fill your bowl with fruit. Quick – eat it up before it melts!

Don't lose your cool

The BIG freeze
Hello, ice to meet you!

Keep ultra cool on a hot, sunny day.
Create icy shapes and turn them ice blue.

Blue cubes

For blue ice cubes, add food colouring to the water before you fill up the tray.

Sugar-coated cooler

Dip the top rim of a glass in some water.

Now dip the rim in a dish of sugar.

The sugar will stick to the glass.

Fill with lemonade and drop in the ice cubes. Look how it turns blue – how refreshing!

Ice sculpture cocktail

Not just cubes – water will freeze into any shape you like. Try a balloon, the bottom of a plastic bottle, or even a rubber glove for some really spooky frozen fingers!

Add food colouring to the water before you freeze it to make coloured ice

Ice tips

• For hand and balloon shapes, make sure you seal the water by tying up the balloon or using a clothes peg on the rubber glove. You may have to cut the balloon and the glove to release them, so make sure you use an old glove.

• Run the shapes under cold water if they are difficult to take out of their moulds.

Rubber glove

Frozen fingers

Rain cloud

Balloon

Jelly mould

Snowball

Floating flower

Plastic bottle base

Iceberg

Plastic bag

watch out!
Shark attack

Grrrrrrrr

Let's move it!

Go, Go, Go!

Keep your cool
What floats and what doesn't? It's a matter of life and death if there are vicious sharks in the water. Quick, get this boat out of here!

Crafty boats

Think or you'll sink! All you need to remember is, if it floats it'll make a boat. You'll need it to float if the sharks are about!

use anything you can find that floats for boat-building materials

To make a basic boat

All you need are two plastic bottles and a plastic food tray. When you have finished, add special features, such as a control deck or a go-faster spoiler.

Carefully make a hole in each corner.

Plastic bottle   Plastic food tray   Plastic bottle   Scissors and string

Tie a piece of string through each hole and around each bottle tightly.

☆ **Ask an adult** to help when you are near water.

Fluttering flags and bunting to liven up your sunny day party.

Bags of flags

Transform plastic carrier bags into festive banners that flutter in the breeze.

28

Start collecting colourful plastic bags

Bags of fun

Every time someone goes shopping in your family, keep the plastic bags. You'll be amazed how useful they can be!

How to make flags from bags

Bags of bunting

All you have to do is make a template in a triangle shape. Cut the triangles out of plastic bags and attach them with string. Have bags of fun!

Cut out a paper triangle template.

Draw a line around the paper.

Cut out lots and lots of colourful triangles.

Bags of flags

Cut a plastic drinks bottle into bands to make the flag support to tape strips of plastic to. Perfect to hang up in a breezy place to flutter in the wind.

☆ **Ask an adult** to help cut the bottle.

Cut out a colourful piece of plastic bag and stick it over the bottle band.

Cut the bottle into 5 cm (2 in) bands.

Cut strips of plastic and tape them to the plastic band.

30

use all sorts of plastic bags to make trillions of triangles

Lay the triangles in a row and place a long piece of string along the bottom.

Tape the string in place.

Fold the plastic over the string and staple it in place.

Wrap the band into a circular shape and attach the ends with tape.

Attach some string to the band and hang it up outside.

31

Streamers on parade

You will need:

• A drinking cup • Garden cane • Plastic bag • Scissors • Glue • Sticky tape

Cut out the base of a cup.

Make two holes in the side for the cane.

Use a sharp pencil to make the holes.

Push the cane through the holes.

Glue the cane in place and add some sticky tack for decoration.

Bring the folded bag up through the bottom of the cup.

Fold the bag so that it is a strip about 4 cm (2 in) wide.

Bring the bag over the cane and tape it in place.

Starting from the bottom, cut the bag into strips about 2 cm (1 in) wide to the base of the cup.

Add some decoration.

Streaming by

By running and running with the streamers in the sunshine, you will make a whooshing sound behind you. When you have finished running, plant them in the ground and let them wave in the breeze.

watch us race with swishing streamers

Party time!

33

Sun catchers

Shimmering, glittering mobiles

twist and turn in the breeze catching the bright sunlight.

34

Silver scraps

Look out for things lying around the house that reflect the sun. Try CDs, gift wrap, and shiny plastic bottles.

How to catch the sun

Jazz up your garden by finding anything that shines, glitters, or shimmers, and make mobiles with it. As they twist and turn in the sunlight they glisten and dance. And on a dull day they will simply cheer up the garden.

Spiral catcher

The basic shape of this sun catcher is a spiral of kitchen foil and a used CD. However with a bit of imagination you can turn it into a real dazzler. Add sequins, shiny buttons, old Christmas decorations, or even double- up the spiral to make an enormous spiral catcher!

String

Twisted foil

CD

1. Cut about a 60 cm (2 ft) length of kitchen foil.

2. Scrunch and twist it up in your hands until it is a solid tube.

3. Twist it around your hand. Add another for a longer spiral.

4. Tie a piece of string to the top of the spiral, then tie the other end around a CD.

Leave some extra string at the top to hang it up.

Decide where you want the CD to hang before you tie it.

Dancing paper plates

The secret to the paper plate catcher is to decorate both sides of the plate, that way whichever way it turns it will sparkle.

1. Draw a zig-zag around a paper plate and cut it out.

Shiny sweet wrappers

2. Now cover it with lots of shiny things.

Foil dish

Sequins

3. Tape some string to the back and add any other shiny things you can find.

Christmas bauble

Bottle-bell mobile

• Take a piece of card – 3 cm (1 in) across – poke a hole through the middle of it, and thread it half way along a piece of string. Fix it in place.

• Thread a button below it.

• Now attach some decorations such as CDs, baubles, and anything else that shimmers.

• Now simply thread the bottle-bell through the top of the string and it will sit on the card.

Piece of card

Button

String

CD

Bauble

How to make the bottle-bell

1. Cut the bottom off a drinks bottle.

2. Cut 2 cm ($\frac{1}{2}$ in) strips about two-thirds of the way up the bottle.

3. Roll each strip up with your fingers and they will curl.

These old, shiny decorations are perfect. Squeeze two together and they will stay attached!

Let's sparkle in the sunlight

Thread it through until it sits on the card.

4. Thread the string through the neck of the bottle.

Tiny camps for tiny toys

A camp within a camp. On the edge of your garden camp sits another tiny adventure world. Let's get building!

This way for the building site

Portable campsite

Camps on trays are very useful as you can take them inside if it rains. You could use anything to decorate your landscape, you could even lay a little soil and plant some small flowers in it. Work out what you would like best in a campsite and get building!

Tiny Swing

Straw

2 x paperclips
bent out of
shape.

Peg

Cardboard

Peg

Tape the paperclips to the cardboard
to make the seat. Then hook them
over the straw.

Twig frame tent

Collect up some small twigs,
make the frame, and hang a
piece of material over it.

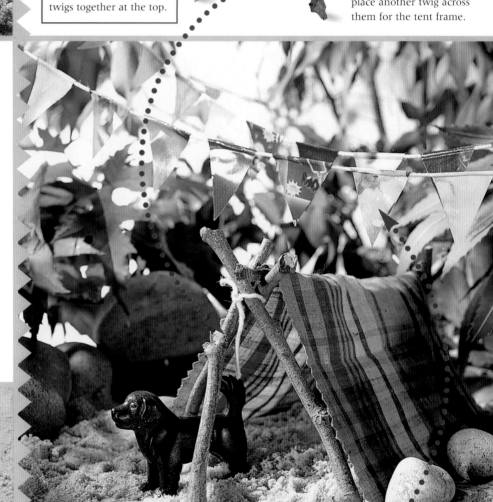

Tie tightly
with string.

For the legs, tie three
twigs together at the top.

Stand the two ends up and
place another twig across
them for the tent frame.

Baby bunting

Collect some pieces
of coloured paper
and a long piece
of string.

Cut the paper into
diamond shapes.

Glue one side of
the diamond.

Fold it over the string with the glue
on the inside to form a triangle.

Get camping!

Put it together! Take a tray and fill it will sand, gravel, or soil. Find some pebbles or rocks and place them around the edge. Now use your imagination to fill it with teeny, tiny camping gear.

I can't wait to move in!

Pebbles create a good landscape.

Use pebbles to keep the material down

A tiny picnic stand made with three twigs and a bottle top.

Sponge fish

A pond made out of a food container.

You could use sand as your base

Casting Shadows

View the world from some strange angles using shadows from the sun, and then capture them on camera.

Snap happy! Don't be camera shy!

You will need:

- A camera – disposable cameras are handy
- Some willing models
- Your imagination
- Lots of bright sunshine

Call me Turkey!

Special effects

Hand shadows against a wall are great, but why not use your whole body to create some really strange shadow effects. You could even base a story around your shadow photos.

Fun in the Sun — what can we play?

Make a water bomb

1 Fold a square piece of paper along the dotted lines as shown here.

2 Turn the paper over and fold inwards to make a triangle.

3 Fold the outside corners to meet the central point. Turn the paper over and repeat.

4 Now you have a diamond shape.

Fold the two side corners into the middle of the shape.

Turn over and repeat on the other side.

5 Fold the top corner flaps down and poke into the gaps made by step 4. Turn over and repeat the other side.

6 Now hold the shape gently and blow into the hole at the top.

Blow

It should puff out nicely. Now fill it with water through the hole and throw!

Races

Think you're fast? Well, set up some races to see if you can beat your friends. Start off with straight running races, then try relay races, where you form teams and as one person in the team finishes they touch the next person to carry on.

Games with paper, games with balls, games with water, fun in the sun.

Drink on the go....

No cup handy? Here's a quick way to make one out of a piece of square paper.

1 Fold a square piece of paper in half to make a triangle shape.

2 Fold the corner of the triangle up as shown here.

3 Repeat with the other corner.

4 Fold down the top. Turn over and repeat on the other side.

Slurp!

Shadow tag

Instead of touching each other, as in a game of tag, try jumping on each other's shadow. The person chasing has to try to stand on someone's shadow, when they do that person becomes the chaser. You won't find it easy!

You can't catch me!

Here, catch the ball

Obstacle course

Ask an adult for some bits and bobs from around the garden or house that you can use to set up an obstacle course in the garden. Then time each other to finish it.

Jump over the broom, hop on one leg through the tyres, and kick the ball!

Football skills

The garden is the best place to brush up on your football skills – you are less likely to cause any damage! How many times can you keep the ball up using your knees?

45

Blowing bubbles

Make your own bubble mixture, then search your house for things that you think you could blow bubbles through. You can make lots and lots of tiny bubbles or huge giant ones.

Gently blow through the gaps.

Bubble recipe
Use one large cup of washing-up liquid, then mix in two large jugs of water.

Mix the recipe in a big bowl

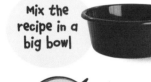

what makes a good bubble?

Bend wire or old coathangers into shapes to make you own blowers.

Boing

46

then more games, and when you have finished, play even more!

water squirters

One of the most refreshing ways to cool off in the hot sun is to get completely soaked. So get into your swimming clothes and if you don't have a water squirter, then try making one. Plastic bottles are good, but try old shampoo or washing up liquid bottles too. It's all a matter of experimenting.

Ball games

Any ball games are fun. If you have a lot of friends with you then split into teams and compete against each other. Choose a team captain and make sure you agree about the rules before you start. If you want to play football, set up goal posts using bits and pieces found around your garden.

Hide and seek

Ask a friend to count to 50 and find the best hiding place you can in the garden. Keep very still and very quiet and wait until the seeker finds you. The first to be found is the seeker next time round. Sometimes the best hiding places are the most obvious ones. Remember, keep still!

☆ **Ask an adult** to watch you when you are around water.

Here, catch the ball

. . . and hide-aways

A secret camp in the garden is a great way to keep out of the sun and to form a club. For an instant and temporary camp, try using chairs with a blanket draped over them and one on the floor. Fill it with cushions.

Happy sunny days!

47

INDEX

ACKNOWLEDGEMENTS

With thanks to the models . . .
Eleanor Bates, Luke Bower,
Charlotte, Billy and James Bull, Seriye
Ezigwe, Max, Guy and Imogen Lowrie
for being little rays of sunshine

The publishers would like to thank the
following for their kind permission to
reproduce their photographs: (Abbreviations
key: t=top, b=bottom, r=right, c=centre)

43tl Stuart McClymont, 43tr Corbis: Richard
Ransier;, 43bl Getty Images: Robert Stahl;
44r Corbis: Peter N. Fox; 45c Getty Images:
Robert Stahl; 46r Corbis: Peter Steiner; 47l
Corbis: Dirk Douglass.

All other images © Dorling Kindersley.
For further information see:
www.dkimages.com